Microsoft Excel 2013 Essentials

Michelle N. Halsey

Contents

Chapter 1 – Opening Excel

Welcome to the new and improved Microsoft Excel 2013. This chapter will teach you how to open Microsoft Excel files and create new ones. First, we will learn how to open Microsoft Excel. You will learn how to open files from the Recent list or other files. Then you will learn how to create a blank workbook or a workbook from a template.

Opening Excel

To open Excel in Windows 8, use the following procedure.

Step 1: From the Start page, select the Excel 2013 icon.

Use this procedure if using Windows 7:

Step 1: Select the Start icon from the lower left side of the screen.

Step 2: Select **All Programs**.

Step 3: Select **Microsoft Office**.

Step 4: Select **Microsoft Office Excel 2013**.

Using the Recent List

To open a workbook from the Recent list, use the following procedure.

Step 1: Select the workbook that you want to open from the Recent list.

To pin an item on the Recent list, use the following procedure.

Step 1: Click the pin on the right side of the Recent list item. The item moves to the top section of the Recent list.

To unpin an item, click the pin on the right side of the Recent list again. The item returns to the previous location in the Recent list.

Opening Files

To open a workbook, use the following procedure.

Step 1: Select **Open Other Workbooks** from the bottom of the Recent list. Or select **Open** from the Backstage View.

Step 2: Select one of the **Places** you would like to look for the workbook. The default options are Recent Workbooks, your Microsoft SkyDrive location, and your Computer.

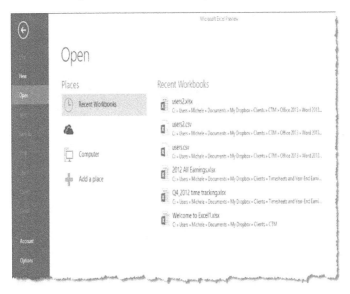

Step 3: To open a document from the SkyDrive or your computer, select **Browse**.

Step 4: In the *Open* dialog box, navigate to the location of the file you want to open. Select it and select **Open**.

Creating a Blank Workbook

To create a blank workbook, use the following procedure.

Step 1: If the Backstage view is not showing, select the **File** tab from the Ribbon. Select **New**.

Step 2: From the **New** tab, or if you have just opened Excel 2013, select **Blank Workbook**.

Creating a Workbook from a Template

To create a blank workbook from a template, use the following procedure.

Step 1: If the Backstage view is not showing, select the **File** tab from the Ribbon. Select **New**.

Step 2: From the **New** tab, or if you have just opened Excel 2013, select the template you want to use.

Step 3: Select **Create**.

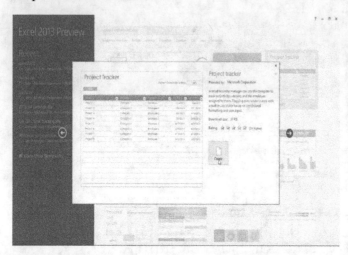

You can use the left and right arrows to review the other templates in the current search.

To search for a template and filter the results, use the following procedure.

Step 1: Select one of the Suggested Search terms or enter a term in the Search box and press Enter.

Step 2: To apply a filter, select the Filter term from the list on the right side of the screen.

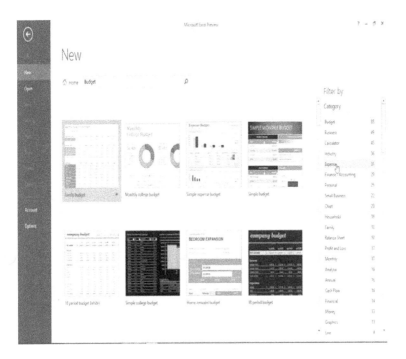

Step 3: To return to the list of templates, select **Home**.

Chapter 2 — Working with the Interface

In this chapter, we will introduce you to the Excel 2013 interface, which uses the Ribbon from the previous two versions of Excel. You will get a closer look at the Ribbon and the Status bar. You will also learn how to manage your Microsoft account right from a new item above the Ribbon. This chapter introduces you to the Backstage view, where all of the functions related to your files live. You will learn how to save files. Finally, we will look at closing files and closing the application.

Understanding the Interface

Explore the Excel interface, including the Ribbon, the formula bar, the worksheet area, the Quick Access toolbar, and the Status bar.

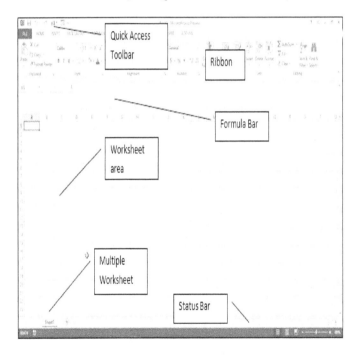

Each Tab in the Ribbon contains many tools for working with your workbook. To display a different set of commands, click the Tab name. Buttons are organized into groups according to their function.

The Quick Access toolbar appears at the top of the Excel window. It provides you with one-click shortcuts to commonly used functions, like save, undo, and redo.

We will discuss the Formula bar more in Chapter 6.

The Status bar shows if any macros are currently running. It also allows you to quickly change your view or zoom of the workbook.

To zoom in or out, use the following procedure.

Step 1: Click the minus sign in the Status bar to zoom out. Click the plus sign in the Status bar to zoom in. You can also drag the slider to adjust the zoom.

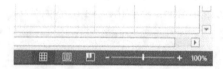

You can also click on the number percentage to open the *Zoom* dialog box.

About Your Account and Feedback

Explore the account options, use the following procedure.

Step 1: Click on the arrow next to the name to change the photo, open the profile information, see the account setting for the current user, or to sign in as a different user.

To send feedback to Microsoft, use the following procedure.

Step 1: Select the Smile icon at the top right corner of the screen.

Step 2: Select Send a Smile or Send a Frown.

Step 3: Enter the information requested in the Microsoft Office Feedback dialog. Select **Send**.

Using Backstage View

Explore the Backstage View, use the following procedure.

Step 1: Select the **File** tab on the Ribbon.

Excel displays the Backstage View, open to the Info tab by default. A sample is illustrated below.

Understanding Worksheets

To move the active cell, point out the highlighted row and column for the active cell, as well as the name of that cell in the Name box.

To insert a new worksheet, use the following procedure.

Step 1: Click the **New Sheet** plus sign.

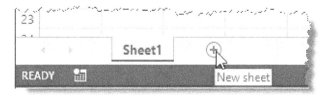

Excel opens the new worksheet to the first cell, so that you can begin entering data right away. You can rename the worksheet if needed.

To rename a worksheet, use the following procedure.

Step 1: Right click on the sheet tab and select **Rename** from the context menu.

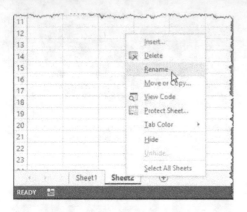

Step 2: Enter the new name over the highlighted text.

To switch to a different worksheet, use the following procedure.

Step 1: Click on the worksheet tab that you want to view.

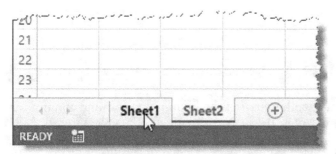

To move a worksheet, use the following procedure.

Step 1: Click on the worksheet tab that you want to move and drag it to the new location in the workbook.

Saving Files

To save a workbook that has not been previously saved, use the following procedure.

Step 1: Select the **File** tab on the Ribbon.

Step 2: Select the **Save** command in the Backstage View.

Step 3: Select the **Place** where you want to save the workbook.

Step 4: If you choose your SkyDrive, you can select the **Documents** folder. If you choose your Computer, select your **Current Folder** or one of your **Recent Folders**. Or in either place, you can choose **Browse** to select a new location.

Step 5: The *Save As* dialog opens. Enter a **File Name**, and if desired, navigate to a new location to store the file. Select **Save**.

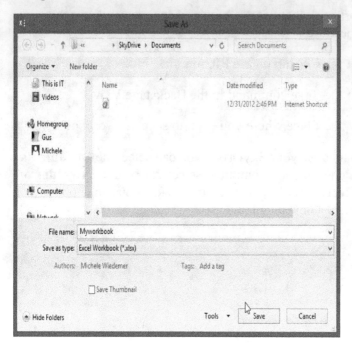

Closing Files vs. Closing Excel

To close a file, use the following procedure.

Step 1: Select the **File** tab from the Ribbon.

Step 2: Select **Close** from The Backstage View.

If you have not saved your file, you will see the following message.

To close the application (if only one workbook is open), use the following procedure.

Step 1: Click the X at the top right corner of the window.

Chapter 3 – Your First Worksheet

In this chapter, you will start entering data into a worksheet, including using flash fill and auto fill to quickly populate the information you need to store in your worksheet. You will also learn about editing data, including checking your spelling. Since you probably do not want to move all of those rows or columns when you realize that you forgot one, you will also learn how to add rows and columns.

Entering Data

Review how a long label will overlap to the next column. In the following example, "Car Payment" is too long for the column width.

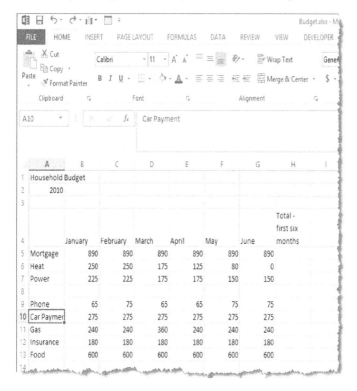

To widen a column, use the following procedure.

Step 1: Click on the column you want to widen. Notice the cursor changes to a cross with double arrows. The screen tips indicate how wide in pixels the column currently is.

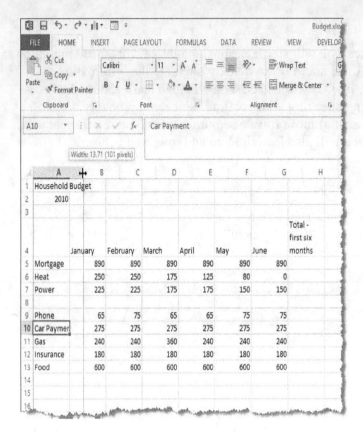

	A	B	C	D	E	F	G	H
1	Household Budget							
2	2010							
3								
4		January	February	March	April	May	June	Total - first six months
5	Mortgage	890	890	890	890	890	890	
6	Heat	250	250	175	125	80	0	
7	Power	225	225	175	175	150	150	
8								
9	Phone	65	75	65	65	75	75	
10	Car Paymer	275	275	275	275	275	275	
11	Gas	240	240	360	240	240	240	
12	Insurance	180	180	180	180	180	180	
13	Food	600	600	600	600	600	600	
14								
15								
16								

Step 2: Drag the border to the new width

Using Auto Fill

To create a list using AutoFill, use the following procedure. This example creates new columns in the Budget worksheet to cover the second six months.

Step 1: Create a new column heading with the text "July" in cell J4.

Step 2: Select that cell to make it active. Excel displays a handle around the cell.

Step 3: Drag the handle across the columns. Excel displays a screen tip showing what AutoFill will place in those cells.

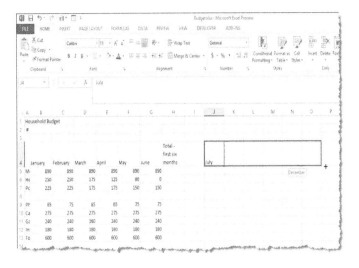

Step 4: Release the mouse button at the end of the range.

Editing Data

Explore the relationship between the active cell and the Formula Bar.

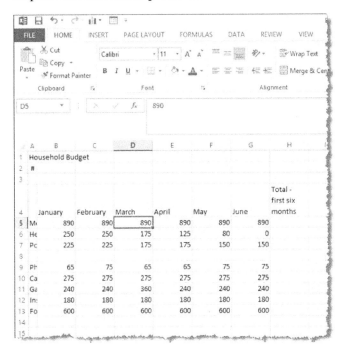

Checking Your Spelling

Explore the Spell Checker, use the following procedure.

Step 1: Select the **Spelling** tool on the **Review** tab of the Ribbon.

Excel opens the **Spelling** dialog box and begins indicating any spelling errors.

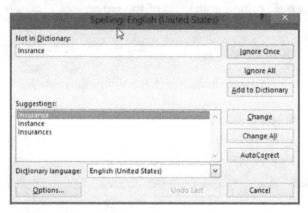

Step 2: Highlight the correct spelling and select Change. If the correct spelling is not listed, you can correct the spelling by editing the text in the **Not in Dictionary** field.

Adding Rows and Columns

To add a new row, use the following procedure.

Step 1: Highlight the row below where you want to insert a row. Click to the left of the row number to highlight the whole row.

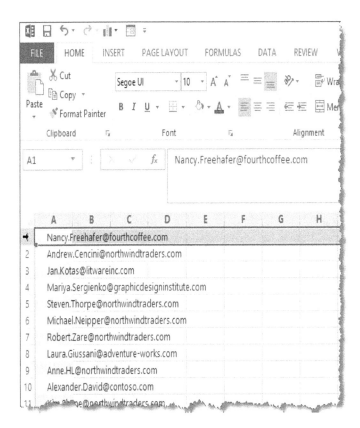

Step 2: Select Insert Sheet Rows from the Ribbon.

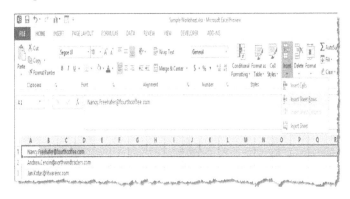

Using Flash Fill

To use flash fill, use the following procedure.

Step 1: Enter Nancy in the First Name cell of the first row.

Step 2: Enter Andrew in the First Name cell of the second row.

Step 3: When Excel displays the remaining list, press Enter to accept.

	A	B	C
1	Email Address	First Name	Last Name
2	Nancy.Freehafer@fourthcoffee.com	Nancy	
3	Andrew.Cencini@northwindtraders.com	Andrew	
4	Jan.Kotas@litwareinc.com	Jan	
5	Mariya.Sergienko@graphicdesigninstitute.com	Mariya	
6	Steven.Thorpe@northwindtraders.com	Steven	
7	Michael.Neipper@northwindtraders.com	Michael	
8	Robert.Zare@northwindtraders.com	Robert	
9	Laura.Giussani@adventure-works.com	Laura	
10	Anne.HL@northwindtraders.com	Anne	
11	Alexander.David@contoso.com	Alexander	
12	Kim.Shane@northwindtraders.com	Kim	
13	Manish.Chopra@northwindtraders.com	Manish	
14	Gerwald.Oberleitner@northwindtraders.com	Gerwald	
15	Amr.Zaki@northwindtraders.com	Amr	
16	Yvnonne.McKay@northwindtraders.com	Yvnonne	
17	Amanda.Pinto@northwindtraders.com	Amanda	
18			

Step 4: Notice the icon that appears with a context menu of additional options.

28

Chapter 4 – Viewing Excel Data

Excel offers several options for viewing your worksheets. This chapter will provide an overview of the different views that are available. It also explains how to switch views and create a custom view. This chapter covers how to use the Zoom feature. Finally, this chapter discusses how to switch between different open files.

An Overview of Excel's Views

Explain the different view options in Excel.

• Normal is the view used for entering data.

• Page Break Preview allows you to adjust where the page breaks occur. You can drag the blue border to a new location for columns or rows to adjust the page breaks.

• Page Layout view displays what the data will look like when printed. You can use Page Layout view to add headers and footers to your worksheets.

Explore the **View** tab on the Ribbon.

Explore the view options on the Status bar.

Switching Views

Explore the Page Break Preview, use the following procedure.

Step 1: Select the **View** tab from the Ribbon.

Step 2: Select the **Page Break Preview** tool.

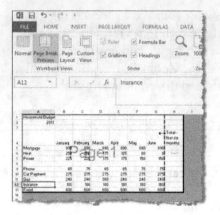

Investigate what happens if you move the blue borders.

Explore the Page Layout View, use the following procedure.

Step 1: Select the **View** tab.

Step 2: Select the **Page Layout** tool.

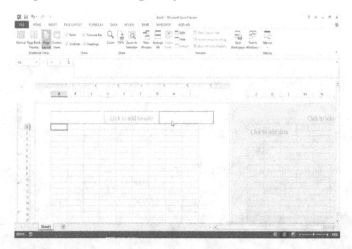

There are three areas for the header and the footer. Practice entering header content in the left, middle, and right of the header and/or footer.

Using Zoom

To zoom to a selection, use the following procedure.

Step 1: Highlight the area you want to view larger.

Step 2: Select the **Zoom to Selection** tool from the **View** tab on the Ribbon.

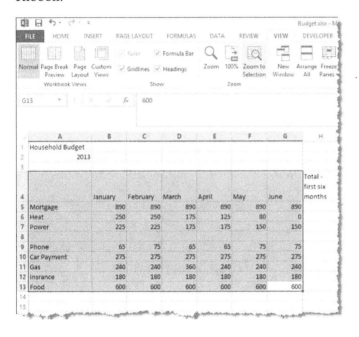

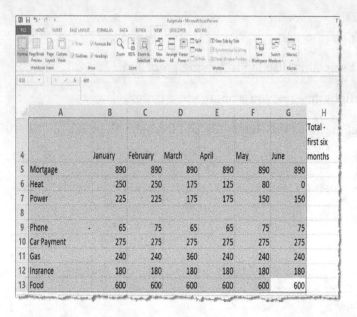

	A	B	C	D	E	F	G	H
								Total - first six months
4		January	February	March	April	May	June	
5	Mortgage	890	890	890	890	890	890	
6	Heat	250	250	175	125	80	0	
7	Power	225	225	175	175	150	150	
8								
9	Phone	65	75	65	65	75	75	
10	Car Payment	275	275	275	275	275	275	
11	Gas	240	240	360	240	240	240	
12	Insrance	180	180	180	180	180	180	
13	Food	600	600	600	600	600	600	

Step 3: Select **100%** from the View tab on the Ribbon to return to the default zoom.

Creating Custom Views

To create a custom view, use the following procedure.

Step 1: Select **Custom Views** from the **View** tab on the Ribbon.

Excel opens the *Custom Views* dialog box.

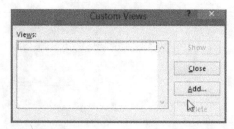

Step 2: Select **Add** to open the *Add View* dialog box.

Step 3: Enter the **Name** of your view.

Step 4: Check the **Print Settings** box to include the print settings in your custom view.

Step 5: Check the **Hidden rows, columns and filter settings** to include those in your custom view.

Step 6: Select **OK**.

To apply a custom view, use the following procedure.

Step 1: Select **Custom Views** from the **View** tab on the Ribbon.

Step 2: Highlight the View you want to apply and select **Show**.

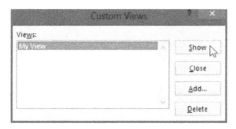

Switching Between Open Files

To switch from one worksheet to another, use the following procedure.

Step 1: Select the **Switch Windows** tool from the **View** tab on the Ribbon. Select the worksheet you want to view from the list.

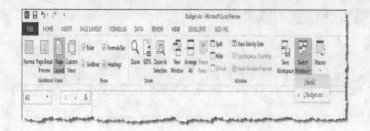

Chapter 5 – Building Formulas

The backbone of Excel is its ability to perform calculations. There are two ways to set up calculations in Excel: using formulas or using functions. Formulas are mathematical expressions that you build yourself. You need to follow proper math principles in order to obtain the expected answer. Building the formula is simply a matter of combining the proper cell addresses with the correct operators in the right order. This chapter will explore how to build, edit, and copy formulas. This chapter will also explain the difference between relative and absolute references. Finally, this chapter will explain how to use the Status Bar to perform simple calculations. We will explore functions in the next chapter.

The Math Basics of Excel

Review the different types of operators.

The Arithmetic operators are:

- Plus Sign (+) – Adds values
- Minus Sign (-) – Subtracts values
- Asterisk (*) – Multiplies values
- Forward slash (/) – Divides values
- Percent sign (%) – Finds the percentage of a value
- Caret (^(– Exponentiation – Finds the exponential value

The Comparison operators are:

- Equals (=) sign – Equates values
- Greater than (>) sign – Indicates that one value is greater than the other
- Less than sign (<) – Indicates that one value is less than the other
- Greater than or equal to (>=) signs – Indicates that one value is greater than or equal to the other
- Less than or equal to (<=) signs – Indicates that one value is less than or equal to the other
- Not Equal (<>) – Indicates that values are not equal

Text concatenation allows you to combine text from different cells into a single piece of text. The operator is the **&** sign.

The reference operators combine a range of cells to use together in an operation. The reference operators are:

- Colon (:) – A Range operator that produces a reference to all of the cells between the references on either side of the colon
- Comma (,) – A Union operator that combines multiple range references
- Space – An intersection operator that returns a reference to the cells common to the ranges in the formula

Building a Formula

To enter a formula to calculate the Total Value in the sample worksheet, use the following procedure.

Step 1: Select the Total Value column for the first product (cell D4).

Step 2: Enter the = sign to begin the formula.

Step 3: Select cell B4 to use it as the first value in the formula. Excel enters the reference as part of the formula.

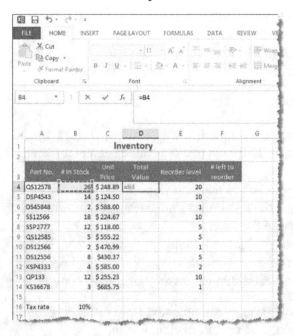

Step 4: Enter the * sign.

Step 5: Click on cell C4 to use it as the second value in the formula. Excel enters the references as part of the formula.

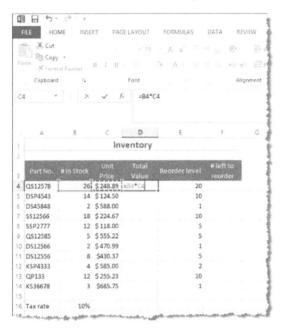

Step 6: Press **ENTER** to complete the formula. Excel moves to the next row and performs the calculations in the formula.

The following illustration shows the answer to the calculation in the cell, and since the cell is active, you can see the formula in the Formula bar.

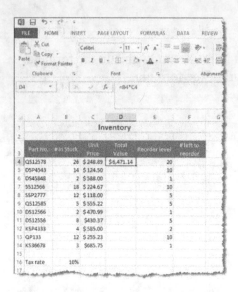

Part No.	# In Stock	Unit Price	Total Value	Reorder level	# left to reorder
QS12578	26	$248.89	$6,471.14	20	
DSP4543	14	$124.50		10	
DS45848	2	$588.00		1	
SS12566	18	$224.67		10	
SSP2777	12	$118.00		5	
QS12585	5	$555.22		5	
DS12566	2	$470.99		1	
DS12556	8	$430.37		5	
KSP4333	4	$585.00		2	
QP133	12	$255.23		10	
KS36678	3	$685.75		1	
Tax rate	10%				

Editing a Formula

To edit a formula, use the following procedure. The following example uses an incorrect cell reference in a formula.

Step 1: Select the cell with the formula you want to correct to make it active.

Step 2: Select the Formula Bar. Excel highlights the cell references in the current formula.

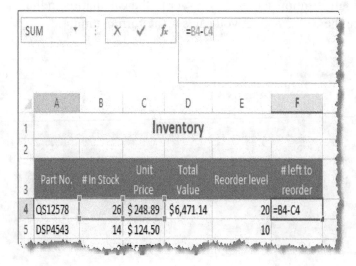

Step 3: Highlight the operator or cell references and either type over with the correct reference or operator, or select the correct cell to replace a cell reference.

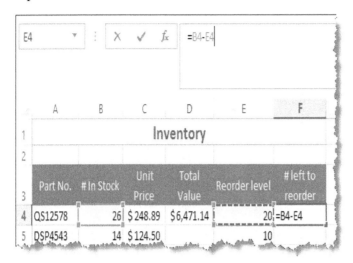

Step 4: Press ENTER to complete the formula. Excel calculates the formula and moves to the next row.

Copying a Formula

To copy and paste a formula, use the following procedure.

Step 1: Select the cell with the formula you want to copy. You can also click on the cell and use the keyboard shortcut: **CTRL + C**.

Step 2: Select **Copy** from the **Home** tab on the Ribbon.

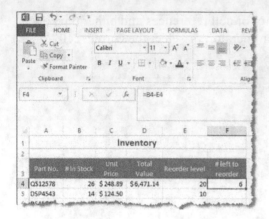

Excel highlights the cell whose contents you are copying. This will remain highlighted until you finish pasting, in case you want to paste the cell contents more than once.

Select the cell where you want to copy the formula. Excel displays a number of paste options. To paste a formula, select **Paste** or **Paste formula**. Note that as you hover your mouse over the paste options, the rest of the context menu is dimmed. You can also select the cell and use the keyboard shortcut: **CTRL + V**.

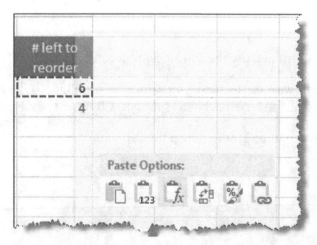

Step 1: You can repeat the paste as many times as desired. Or you can highlight multiple cells at once before pasting to repeat the paste for all highlighted cells.

Step 2: Press **ENTER** to stop pasting.

Relative vs. Absolute References

To copy a formula with an absolute reference, use the following procedure.

Step 1: Create a new column labeled Taxes.

Step 2: Select the Taxes column for the first product (cell E4).

Step 3: Enter the = sign to begin the formula.

Step 4: Select cell B16 to use it as the first value in the formula. Excel enters the reference as part of the formula. Use the Formula Bar to enter dollar signs before the column and the row (i.e., B16).

Step 5: Enter * and the relative reference in the Total Value column.

Step 6: Press **ENTER** to complete the formula. Excel moves to the next row and performs the calculations in the formula.

Copy the formula for the other products and select some of them to see the results.

Using the Status Bar to Perform Calculations

To customize the Status Bar, use the following procedure.

Step 1: Right click on the Status Bar to see a list of Functions that can be displayed. For this example, select MIN and MAX.

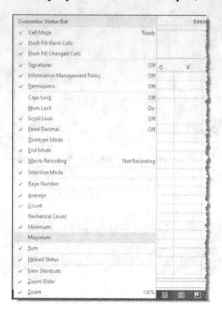

Step 2: Press **ESC** or click elsewhere in the worksheet to close the **Customize Status Bar** list.

Explore the calculations performed when you highlight a group of cells.

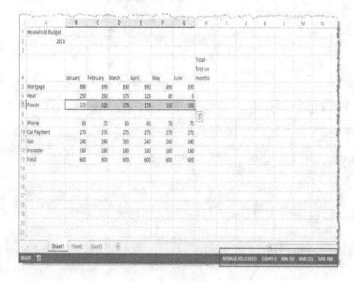

Chapter 6 – Using Excel Functions

This chapter introduces Excel functions, which are a little like templates for common formulas. There are many different types of functions. First, we will look at the SUM function. You will learn about using AutoComplete for entering formulas. We will look at other basic common functions as well. We will take a look at the Formulas tab introduced in the Ribbon for Excel 2007. Finally, we will take a look at the function names.

Formulas vs. Functions

To open the Insert Function dialog box, use the following procedure.

Step 1: Select the **Insert Function** tool right next to the Formula Bar.

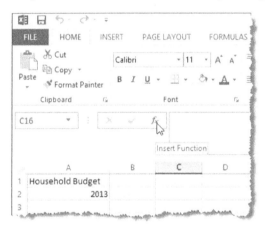

Investigate the different categories and functions in the *Insert Function* dialog box. Point out the bottom part of the screen where the syntax and description of the function appear.

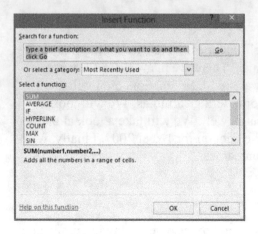

Using the SUM Function

Review how to use a SUM function to add the total for each category in the sample file, use the following procedure.

Step 1: Select the Total –First Six Months column for the first category (cell H5).

Step 2: Select the **AutoSum** tool in the Editing Group on the **Home** tab of the Ribbon.

Step 3: Excel enters the function with a default selection of the cell references you want to use in the function highlighted.

	A	B	C	D	E	F	G	H	I	J
1	Household Budget									
2		2013								
3										
4		January	February	March	April	May	June	Total - first six months		
5	Mortgage	890	890	890	890	890	890	=SUM(B5:G5)		
6	Heat	250	250	175	125	80	0	SUM(number1, [number2], ...)		
7	Power	225	225	175	175	150	150			

Step 4: If the cell references are not accurate, you can drag the highlighted area to include additional cells or remove cells you do not want used in the function.

Step 5: Press **ENTER** to complete the function.

Excel performs the calculation and moves to the next row. In the following illustration, the cell with the function is active, so that you can see the function syntax in the Formula Bar and the result in the cell.

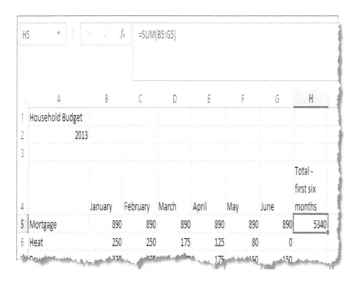

Using AutoComplete

To use the AutoComplete feature, use the following procedure.

Step 1: Begin typing the SUM function. As soon as you type the Equals sign and the letter S, Excel displays a possible list of matching functions.

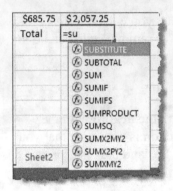

Step 2: To select the SUM Function from the list, double-click on the SUM function.

Step 3: Excel enters the function, but you must still enter the arguments. You can simply click on multiple cells, or click and drag to select a cell range. You can also type in the cell references.

Step 4: Enter the final parenthesis mark to end the function.

Step 5: Press ENTER to enter the function in the cell.

Using Other Basic Excel Functions

Review how to use the AVERAGE function as an example of another function, use the following procedure.

Step 1: Add a new label in column I: Average.

Step 2: Select the cell in the Average column for the first category.

Step 3: Select the arrow next to the SUM function on the Home tab of the Ribbon to see the list of other common functions.

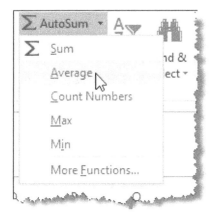

Step 4: Select **Average**.

Excel enters the function with the most likely cell references.

4	January	February	March	April	May	June	Total - first six months	Average
5 Mortgage	890	890	890	890	890	890	5340	=AVERAGE(B5:H5)
6 Heat	250	250	175	125	80	0		AVERAGE(number1, [number2] ...)
7 Power	225	225	175	175	150	150		

Step 5: Replace the cell references so that cell H5 is not included in the average.

4	January	February	March	April	May	June	Total - first six months	Average
5 Mortgage	890	890	890	890	890	890	5340	=AVERAGE(B5:G5)
6 Heat	250	250	175	125	80	0		AVERAGE(number1, [number2] ...)
7 Power	225	225	175	175	150	150		

Step 6: Press **ENTER** to complete the function.

Understanding the Formulas Tab

Explore the **Formulas** tab on the Ribbon.

Understanding Function Compatibility

Explore the icons that appear when entering a function name. The old names have a yellow warning triangle next to them.

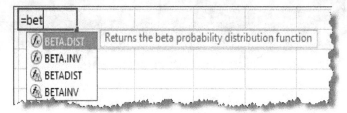

Chapter 7 – Using Quick Analysis

The new Quick Analysis tools allow you to easily preview and apply a number of formatting, charts, totals, tables, and spark lines features to your data. We will first look at the formatting tools. You will also learn about the recommended charts available in Quick Analysis. Next, we will look at the totals tools that include formulas that automatically calculate totals for you. We will also look at the tables available with Quick Analysis. Once you have your data in table format, you can use a number of sorting and filtering tools, which we will also discuss in this chapter. Finally, you will learn how to create spark lines.

Formatting Data

To apply Quick Analysis formatting, use the following procedure.

Step 1: Select the table (A1 to D16) in the sample worksheet.

Step 2: Select the icon that appears at the bottom right of the table.

	A	B	C	D	E
1	Company	Industry	Q1 Sales	Q2 Sales	
2	A. Datum Corporation	Tech	$ 195,449	$ 746,907	
3	Adventure Works	Travel	$ 123,721	$ 733,396	
4	Blue Yonder Airlines	Travel	$ 934,763	$ 246,554	
5	City Power & Light	Utilities	$ 299,293	$ 674,295	
6	Coho Vineyard	Beverage	$ 228,783	$ 659,385	
7	Contoso, Ltd	Misc	$ 239,219	$ 287,989	
8	Contoso Pharmaceuticals	Medical	$ 371,570	$ 644,368	
9	Consolidated Messenger	Tech	$ 579,825	$ 448,399	
10	Fabrikam, Inc.	Utilities	$ 639,630	$ 635,474	
11	Fourth Coffee	Beverage	$ 876,740	$ 567,216	
12	Graphic Design Institute	Education	$ 788,390	$ 540,282	
13	Humongous Insurance	Financial	$ 682,545	$ 577,599	
14	Litware, Inc.	Tech	$ 902,264	$ 206,331	
15	Lucerne Publishing	Misc	$ 905,906	$ 443,552	
16	Margie's Travel	Travel	$ 289,570	$ 843,834	
17					
18					
19					

Step 3: Select the formatting type that you want to use.

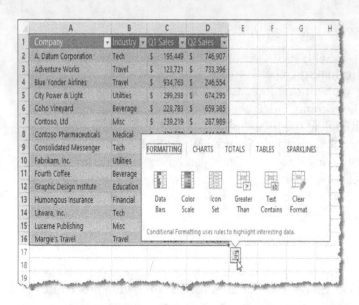

Step 4: For the **Greater Than** option (and some other types of options), enter the cell that contains the value to which you want to compare the others. You can also enter a number or a formula. Also select the formatting you want to use from the drop down list.

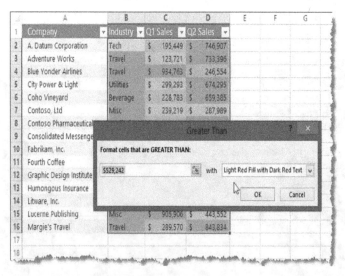

To remove any formatting you have applied, select **Clear format**.

Creating Quick Analysis Charts

To create Quick Analysis charts, use the following procedure.

Step 1: Select the table (A1 to D16) in the sample worksheet.

Step 2: Select the icon that appears at the bottom right of the table.

Step 3: Select **Charts**.

Step 4: Select the chart type that you want to use.

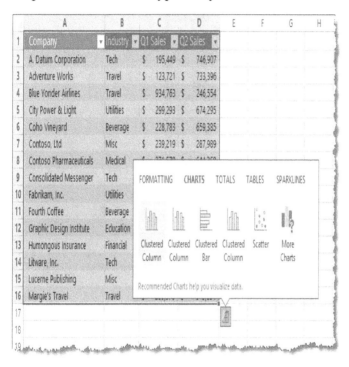

The chart is inserted into your worksheet. If the chart you selected is a PivotChart, it will be created on a separate worksheet.

Calculating Totals

To create Quick Analysis totals, use the following procedure.

Step 1: Select the table (A1 to D16) in the sample worksheet.

Step 2: Select the icon that appears at the bottom right of the table.

Step 3: Select **Totals**.

Step 4: Select the formula that you want to use. Note that there is a right arrow to view additional options.

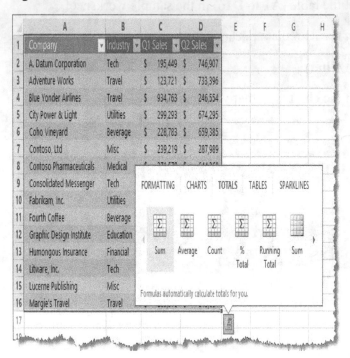

The row or column you selected is inserted into your worksheet.

Creating Quick Analysis Tables

To create Quick Analysis tables, use the following procedure.

Step 1: Select the table (A1 to D16) in the sample worksheet.

Step 2: Select the icon that appears at the bottom right of the table.

Step 3: Select **Tables**.

Step 4: Select the table type that you want to use.

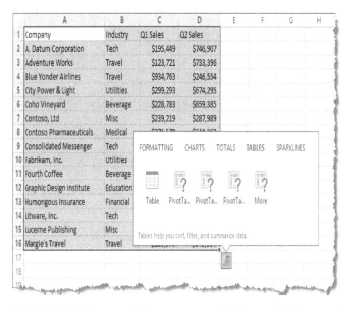

The Table is inserted into your worksheet with formatting and filtering options activated. If the table you selected is a PivotTable, it will be created on a separate worksheet.

Sorting and Filtering Your Data

To sort, use the following procedure.

Step 1: Select the arrow next to the column header that you want to use for sorting or filtering. Or you can select the **Sort & Filter** tool from the Ribbon.

Step 2: Select a sorting option from the list. The list differs, depending on the type of data in the column you selected.

To create a custom sort, use the following procedure.

Step 1: Select one column header you want to use in your sort.

Step 2: Select the **Sort & Filter** tool from the Ribbon.

Step 3: Select **Custom Sort**.

Excel opens the *Sort* dialog box.

Step 4: You can choose the first column by which to sort from the **Sort By** drop down list. The options displayed match the column headers in your worksheet.

Step 5: Select an option from the **Sort On** drop down list. **Values** is selected by default.

Step 6: Select an **Order** from the drop down list.

Step 7: To add another column to your sort, select **Add Level**. Repeat steps 4, 5, and 6 for the next sorting level. You can **Delete the Level**, **Copy a Level**, and rearrange the order of the sorting levels by using the up or down arrows.

Step 8: Select **OK** when you have finished setting up your sort to see the results.

To apply a simple filter, use the following procedure.

Step 1: Select the arrow next to the column header for the column including the value you want to filter.

Step 2: To select a simple filter based on your type of data, select the option provided above the search box. In the example, below, select **Number Filters**. Then select the filter you want to use from the list. Excel will display a dialog box to determine the value to use in your filter.

Step 3: Enter the value you want to use in the dialog box and select **OK**.

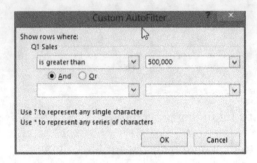

Step 4: To select a simple filter based one or more of your specific values, clear the **Select All** check box to clear the boxes. Check one or more boxes from the items that are taken from your data. Select **OK** to apply the filter.

Excel includes a different small icon in the column header to indicate that a filter has been applied. It only shows the rows that match the filter. The other rows are still present, but hidden.

To clear a filter, use the following procedure.

Step 1: Select the Filter icon next to the column header to open the Sort and Filter context menu.

Step 2: Select **Clear Filter From** to clear the filter.

Using Spark Lines

To create Quick Analysis spark lines, use the following procedure.

Step 1: Select the table (A1 to D16) in the sample worksheet.

Step 2: Select the icon that appears at the bottom right of the table.

Step 3: Select **Spark lines**.

Step 4: Select the type of mini chart that you want to use.

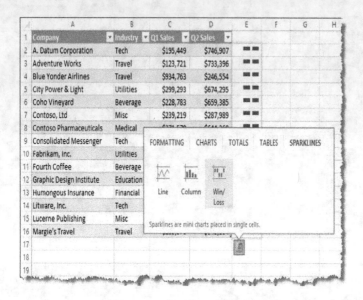

	A	B	C	D	E	F	G	H
1	Company	Industry	Q1 Sales	Q2 Sales				
2	A. Datum Corporation	Tech	$195,449	$746,907				
3	Adventure Works	Travel	$123,721	$733,396				
4	Blue Yonder Airlines	Travel	$934,763	$246,554				
5	City Power & Light	Utilities	$299,293	$674,295				
6	Coho Vineyard	Beverage	$228,783	$659,385				
7	Contoso, Ltd	Misc	$239,219	$287,989				
8	Contoso Pharmaceuticals	Medical						
9	Consolidated Messenger	Tech						
10	Fabrikam, Inc.	Utilities						
11	Fourth Coffee	Beverage						
12	Graphic Design Institute	Education						
13	Humongous Insurance	Financial						
14	Litware, Inc.	Tech						
15	Lucerne Publishing	Misc						
16	Margie's Travel	Travel						
17								
18								
19								

FORMATTING   CHARTS   TOTALS   TABLES   SPARKLINES

Line   Column   Win/ Loss

Sparklines are mini charts placed in single cells.

Chapter 8 – Formatting Your Data

In this chapter, we will look at how to make your worksheet more appealing by changing the font type and size, alignment, formatting numbers, and by adding color and borders. This chapter also explains how to use the merge feature and how to remove formatting.

Changing the Appearance of Text

To apply formatting to text, use the following procedure.

Step 1: Select one or more cells that you want to format.

Step 2: Right-click to display the context menu, or use the formatting tools on the **Home** tab.

Step 2a: Use the **Font** drop down list to select a new font for the text.

Step 2b: Use the **Font Size** drop down list to select a new font size for the text. Alternatively, you can use the **Increase Font Size** or **Decrease Font Size** tools to adjust the font size a point at a time.

Step 2c: Select **Bold, Italics**, or **Underline** to add these features to your text.

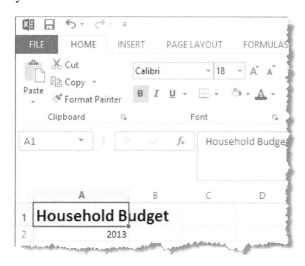

Changing the Appearance of Numbers

To format a number as currency without decimals, use the following procedure.

Step 1: Select the cell or cell range that you want to format.

Step 2: Select the type of number formatting you want to use from the **Number** group drop down list in the **Home** tab of the Ribbon.

Step 3: Select the Decrease Decimal tool (2 times) to remove the decimal places.

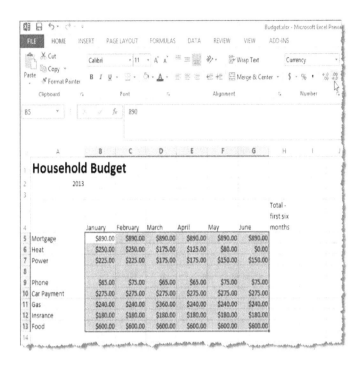

Adding Borders and Fill Color

To add borders, use the following procedure.

Step 1: Highlight the cell or cell range where you want to apply your border.

Step 2: Select the type of border you want to apply from the **Borders** tool on the **Home** tab of the Ribbon.

To apply fill colors, use the following procedure.

Step 1: Highlight the cell or cell range where you want to apply your fill color.

Step 2: Select the color you want to apply from the **Fill Color** tool on the **Home** tab of the Ribbon.

Removing Formatting

To clear formatting, use the following procedure.

Step 1: Select the cell or cell range that you want to clear.

Step 2: Select the **Clear** tool from the **Home** tab on the Ribbon.

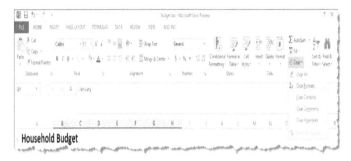

Step 3: Select **Clear Formats**.

Working with Alignment Options

To align cell contents, use the following procedure.

Step 1: Select the cell or cell range that you want to align.

Step 2: Select the type of alignment you want to use from the Alignment group tools in the Home tab of the Ribbon.

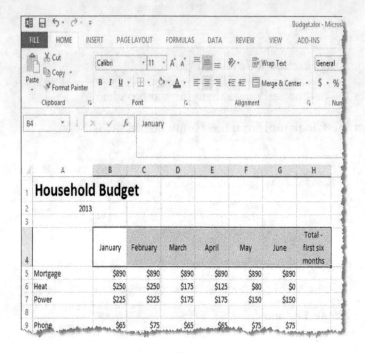

To merge cells, use the following procedure.

Step 1: Highlight the cell range that you want to merge.

Step 2: Select the **Merge** tool from the **Home** tab of the Ribbon.

Step 3: Select **Merge & Center**.

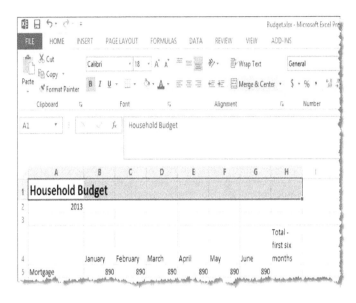

To wrap text, use the following procedure.

Step 1: Select the cell that you would like to wrap.

Step 2: Select **Wrap Text** from the **Home** tab on the Ribbon.

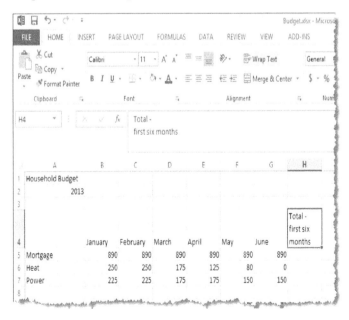

Chapter 9 – Using Styles, Themes, and Effects

In this chapter, you will learn some more advanced formatting options. First, we will discuss table styles and cell styles, including using the *Format Cells* dialog box to apply all types of formatting to your cells at once. This chapter explains conditional formatting. You have seen a little conditional formatting with the Quick Analysis formats. Conditional formatting is simply applying a certain type of formatting to cells that meet certain requirements. Finally, you will learn how to change the theme, colors and fonts, which can help you provide a consistent branding to all of your documents, workbooks, and other office creations.

Using Table Styles and Cell Styles

To apply a table style, use the following procedure.

Step 1: Highlight the cell or cell range where you want to apply your style.

Step 2: Select the **Format as Table** arrow from the **Home** tab on the Ribbon to see the gallery of options.

Step 3: Select the style that you want to apply.

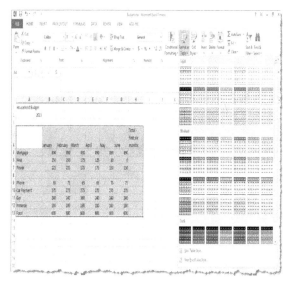

Step 4: In the *Format as Table* dialog box, Excel shows the cell range for your table matching your selection. If you need to change it, you can select a new range of cells. Check the **My Table has Headers** box if applicable. Select **OK**.

The data is now formatted as a table, with filtering options in the column headers.

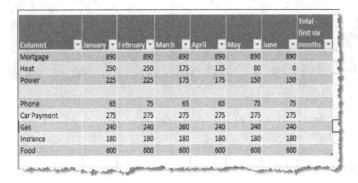

Column1	January	February	March	April	May	June	Total - first six months
Mortgage	890	890	890	890	890	890	
Heat	250	250	175	125	80	0	
Power	225	225	175	175	150	150	
Phone	65	75	65	65	75	75	
Car Payment	275	275	275	275	275	275	
Gas	240	240	360	240	240	240	
Insrance	180	180	180	180	180	180	
Food	600	600	600	600	600	600	

To apply a cell style, use the following procedure.

Step 1: Highlight the cell or cell range where you want to apply your style.

Step 2: Select the **Cell Styles** tool from the **Home** tab of the Ribbon to see the style gallery.

Step 3: Select the style that you want to apply. You can see a preview before you select a style.

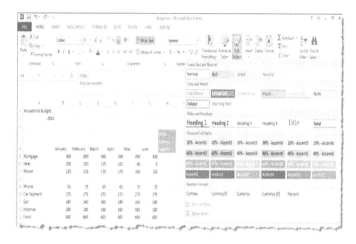

To create a new cell style, use the following procedure.

Step 1: Highlight the cell or cell range where you want to apply your style.

Step 2: Select the Cell Styles tool from the Home tab of the Ribbon to see the style gallery.

Step 3: Select **New Cell Style** to open the Style dialog box.

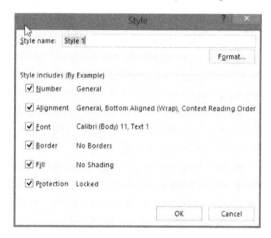

Step 4: Enter a name for the style in the **Style Name** field.

Step 5: Check the **Style Includes** boxes to indicate what formatting features the style should include.

Step 6: Select **Format** to open the **Format Cells** dialog box.

Step 7: Use the *Format Cells* dialog box to indicate each formatting feature for the style. Select **OK** when you have finished indicating all of the formatting features for the style.

Step 7a: The **Number** tab allows you to set number formatting for cells that contain values.

Step 7b: The **Alignment** tab allows you to set text alignment for cells that contain text.

Step 7c: The **Font** tab allows you to set the font for the style.

Step 7d: The **Border** tab allows you to set customized borders for the style.

Step 7e: The **Fill** tab allows you to set customized fill color for the style.

Step 7f: The **Protection** tab allows you to protect the cells from changes if you use the Protection feature.

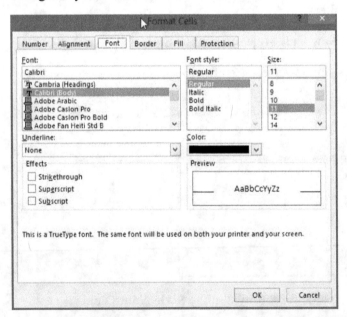

Step 8: Select **OK** to save your style and close the *Style* dialog box.

The new style appears at the top of the Cell Style gallery.

Using Conditional Formatting

To apply conditional formatting, use the following procedure. In this example, we will format all monthly totals in the budget that are over $2500.

Step 1: Highlight the cell or cell range where you want to use conditional formatting.

Step 2: Select the **Conditional Formatting** tool from the **Home** tab on the Ribbon.

Step 3: Select **Highlight Cell Rules**. Select **Greater Than**.

Excel displays the *Greater Than* dialog box to help you complete the conditional formatting rule.

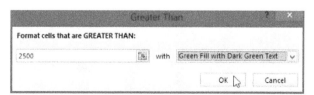

Step 4: Enter 2500 in the left field.

Step 5: Select a formatting option from the right drop down list.

Step 6: Select **OK** to apply the conditional formatting.

	A	B	C	D	E	F	G	H	I
1		Household Budget							
2	2013								
3									
4		January	February	March	April	May	June	Total - first six months	
5	Mortgage	890	890	890	890	890	890	5340	
6	Heat	250	250	175	125	80	0	880	
7	Power	225	225	175	175	150	150	1100	
8								0	
9	Phone	65	75	65	65	75	75	420	
10	Car Payment	275	275	275	275	275	275	1650	
11	Gas	240	240	360	240	240	240	1560	
12	Insrance	180	180	180	180	180	180	1080	
13	Food	600	600	600	600	600	600	3600	
14		2725	2735	2720	2550	2490	2410	15630	
15									

To create a new conditional formatting rule, use the following procedure.

Step 1: Highlight the cell or cell range where you want to use conditional formatting.

Step 2: Select the **Conditional Formatting** tool from the **Home** tab on the Ribbon.

Step 3: Select **New Rule**.

Excel opens the **New Formatting Rule** dialog box.

Step 4: The options in this dialog box differ, based on the **Rule Type** you select. Select the **Rule Type** and follow the prompts to indicate the conditions for when to apply the formatting.

Step 5: Select **Format** to open the **Format Cells** dialog box to create the formatting to apply when the conditions are met.

Step 6: Select **OK** to save your rule and close the **New Formatting Rule** dialog box.

Changing the Theme, Colors, and Fonts

To change the theme, use the following procedure.

Step 1: Select the **Page Layout** tab from the Ribbon.

Step 2: Select **Themes**.

Step 3: Select a new theme from the gallery. You can see a preview of each theme before you apply it.

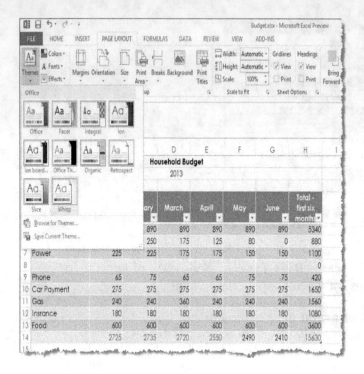

To change the colors, use the following procedure.

Step 1: Select the **Page Layout** tab from the Ribbon.

Step 2: Select **Colors**.

Step 3: Select a new color scheme from the gallery. You can see a preview of each color scheme before you apply it.

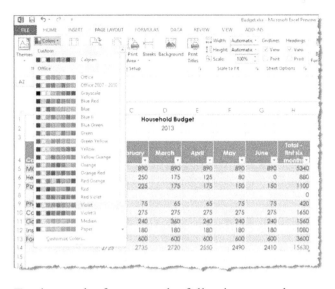

To change the fonts, use the following procedure.

Step 1: Select the **Page Layout** tab from the Ribbon.

Step 2: Select **Fonts**.

Step 3: Select a new font scheme from the gallery. You can see a preview of each font scheme before you apply it.

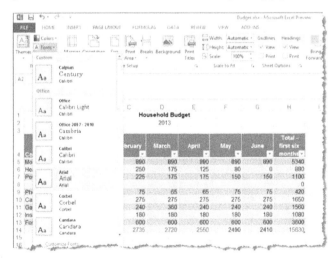

Chapter 10 – Printing and Sharing Your Workbook

This chapter discusses printing your worksheets. First, the chapter covers the Page Layout tab for setting up the worksheet page. Next, the chapter goes into more detail on setting up your pages. The chapter discusses how to use Print Preview. Finally, the chapter explains how to print your worksheets.

An Overview of the Page Layout Tab

Explore the **Page Layout** tab on the Ribbon.

Setting up Your Page

To change the page orientation, use the following procedure.

Step 1: Select the **Page Layout** tab from the Ribbon.

Step 2: Select **Orientation**.

Step 3: Select **Landscape**.

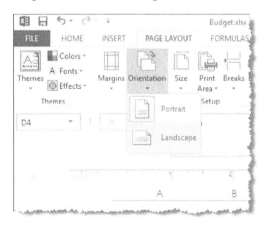

To use custom margins, use the following procedure.

Step 1: Select **Custom Margins** from the **Margins** tool on the **Page Layout** tab of the Ribbon.

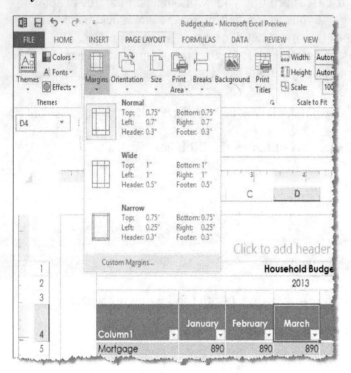

Excel displays the *Page Setup* dialog box.

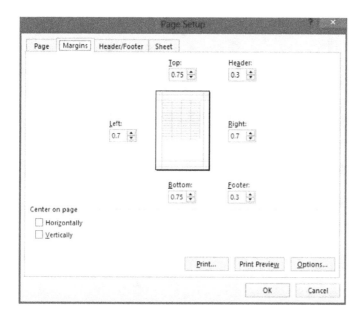

Step 2: Use the up and/or down arrows to control each of the margins (in inches). When have finished, select **OK**.

To insert a page break, use the following procedure.

Step 1: Place your cursor on the row or column where you want the page break to occur. Excel will insert the break above and to the left of your cursor.

Step 2: Select the **Breaks** tool from the **Page Layout** tab on the Ribbon.

Step 3: Select **Insert Page Break**.

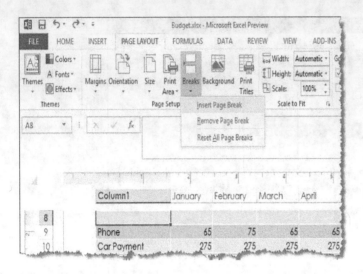

Previewing and Printing Your Workbook

Explore the **Print** tab in the Backstage View.

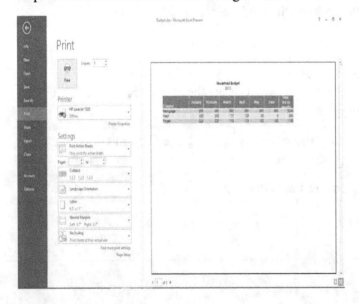

Inviting People

To invite people to the workbook, use the following procedure.

Step 1: Select the **File** tab from the Ribbon to open the Backstage view.

Step 2: Select the **Share** tab.

Step 3: Select **Invite People**.

Step 4: Enter the names or email addresses for the people that you want to invite.

Step 5: Enter a message to include with the invitation.

Step 6: If desired, check the **Require User To Sign-In Before Accessing Document** box to enhance the security of your workbook.

Step 7: Select **Share**.

To get a link for the document, use the following procedure.

Step 1: Select the **File** tab from the Ribbon to open the Backstage view.

Step 2: Select the **Share** tab.

Step 3: Select **Get a Link**.

Step 4: Select the **Create Link** button next to **View Link** or **Edit Link** (or both), depending on what type of editing rights you want to provide. You can copy the link and paste it to another location, such as an email or a blog page.

Step 5: If you want to remove the sharing rights, select **Disable Link**.

E-Mailing Your Workbook

To email an attachment or send a link, use the following procedure.

Step 1: Select the **File** tab on the Ribbon.

Step 2: Select the **Share** tab in the Backstage View.

Step 3: Select **Email**.

Step 4: Select **Send as Attachment** or **Send a Link**.

Step 5: Outlook opens with an email started.

If you select **Send as Attachment**, the name of the document is used as the subject and the document is already attached to the email. Enter the email addresses and any personal message you want to include.

If you select **Send a Link**, the name of the document is used as the subject and the link is included in the body message of the email. Enter the email addresses and any personal message that you want to include.

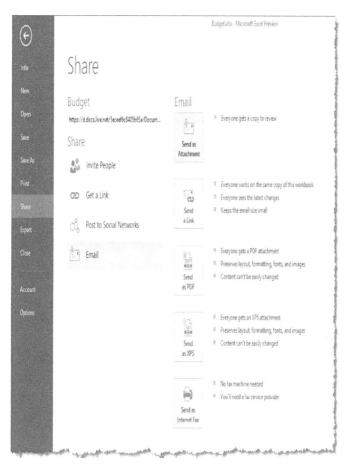

Additional Titles

The Technical Skill Builder series of books covers a variety of technical application skills. For the availability of titles please see https://www.silvercitypublications.com/shop/. Note the Master Class volume contains the Essentials, Advanced, and Expert (when available) editions.

Current Titles

Microsoft Excel 2013 Essentials

Microsoft Excel 2013 Advanced

Microsoft Excel 2013 Expert

Microsoft Excel 2013 Master Class

Microsoft Word 2013 Essentials

Microsoft Word 2013 Advanced

Microsoft Word 2013 Expert

Microsoft Word 2013 Master Class

Microsoft Project 2010 Essentials

Microsoft Project 2010 Advanced

Microsoft Project 2010 Expert

Microsoft Project 2010 Master Class

Microsoft Visio 2010 Essentials

Microsoft Visio 2010 Advanced

Microsoft Visio 2010 Master Class

Coming Soon

Microsoft Access 2013 Essentials

Microsoft Access 2013 Advanced

Microsoft Access 2013 Expert

Microsoft Access 2013 Master Class

Microsoft PowerPoint 2013 Essentials

Microsoft PowerPoint 2013 Advanced

Microsoft PowerPoint 2013 Expert

Microsoft PowerPoint 2013 Master Class

Microsoft Outlook 2013 Essentials

Microsoft Outlook 2013 Advanced

Microsoft Outlook 2013 Expert

Microsoft Outlook 2013 Master Class

Microsoft Publisher 2013 Essentials

Microsoft Publisher 2013 Advanced

Microsoft Publisher 2013 Master Class

Windows 7 Essentials

Windows 8 Essentials

www.ingramcontent.com/pod-product-compliance
Lightning Source LLC
La Vergne TN
LVHW051747050326
832903LV00029B/2766